AF438520

Welcome
to

"A Week in the Word:
12-Week Bible Study Journal"

A Customizable, Inductive Study Guide
to Help You Dig Deep into God's Word
One Passage & One Week at a Time

Heather Erdmann
thebiblebasedlife.com

Copyright © 2022 by Heather Erdmann

All rights reserved. No part of this publication may be reproduced, distributed, or transmitted in any form or by any means, including photocopying, recording, or other electronic or mechanical methods, without the prior written permission of the publisher, except in the case of brief quotations embodied in critical reviews and certain other noncommercial uses permitted by copyright law. For permission requests, write to the publisher, addressed "Attention: Permissions Coordinator," at the address below.

The advice and strategies found within may not be suitable for every situation. This work is sold with the understanding that neither the author nor the publisher is held responsible for the results accrued from the advice in this book.

First Edition

ISBN: 979-8-9861656-7-7

Good Portion Promises
P.O. Box 82
Little Chute, WI 54140

Unless otherwise indicated, all Scripture quotations are taken from the (NASB®) New American Standard Bible®, Copyright © 1960, 1971, 1977, 1995 by The Lockman Foundation. Used by permission. All rights reserved. www.lockman.org

Table of Contents

About this Study

A Week in the Word is an insightful Bible study guide meant to enhance your daily quiet time and help you to dig deeper into any passage of Scripture that you want to study. This easy-to-follow plan will teach you how to better understand and correctly interpret and apply God's Word as you go through the activities each day.

By immersing yourself in one selected passage throughout the week, you will grow in your understanding of the Bible and be able to more fully incorporate what you learn into your daily life. It is designed to help you cover various aspects of a thorough, inductive Bible study—yet in a manageable and enjoyable way.

What exactly does "inductive" mean? In simple terms, it means going from the details to making a broader conclusion. By looking at specific observations, evidence, keywords, and patterns in Scripture, we can better understand the bigger picture.

This study guide will help you find context, meaning, correct interpretation, and most importantly life application as you grow to know and love Him more and then apply what He shows you in your time with Him each day.

Let's sit at the feet of Jesus and learn from Him through His Word, like Mary
did in the Gospel of Luke...

**"but one thing is necessary
Mary has chosen the good portion,
which will not be taken away
from her." (Luke 10:42)**

Daily Plan

Have a more valuable quiet time with the Lord in His Word using this simple
daily system. Each day you will pray, review a weekly memory verse, read the
selected Scripture passage, and then do the corresponding day's activities
(see below) with the reading, followed by a closing prayer.

The schedule is set up to be done Monday-Sunday, but you can start any day
of the week using Day One as your starting point.

Day One (Monday):
- Write out the memory verse
- Study context, genre, author, setting, audience
- Add reading to Bible timeline

Day Two (Tuesday):
- Verse mapping using interlinear (Hebrew/Greek) OR dictionary

Day Three (Wednesday):
- Attributes of God
- Worship with hymn/praise song

Day Four (Thursday):
- Read selection in other trusted versions
- Dig deeper using cross-references

Day Five (Friday):
- Trusted commentaries and/or sermons
- Life application

Days Six & Seven (Saturday & Sunday):
- Review and reflect on the week's study
- Worship in a Bible-based church fellowship

Instructions for How to Do Each Day's Study:

*Please NOTE: This guide is meant to be used with a selected Scripture passage that you choose. (I recommend one Bible chapter or less to make the activities easier to complete and to make your study more focused).

If you prefer a more guided approach, pre-scripted studies are available separately which gives you the weekly passage, memory verse, keywords, praise song, cross-references, etc. It is completely between you and the Lord on what portion of Scripture you would like to explore further each week. You may choose to do a ready-made plan one week, and then your own passage the next. This allows you to customize the guide to best suit your needs.

Every Day:
Start and end with prayer. After your opening prayer, read the selected passage and review your key verse (memory verse) for the week.

Day 1: Context
This is where you will study the context of your passage. This is important because each verse was written at a specific time, for a specific audience. Scripture can never mean to us what it did not mean to its original audience. First, look up the author and recipients (use your study Bible notes, a Bible app, or even Google). Decide the genre(s) of your reading: Historical, Poetry/Wisdom, Gospel, Epistle, Prophecy, etc. This will help with correct interpretation when you understand the style and type of literature in which your passage was written. Examples of genres used in the Bible are given for you in the Appendix. Then, note the setting. What was going on as the passage was happening? You may need to look at the previous verses or headings for help. Lastly, go to the back of this guide and make a note on the timeline at the approximate time this story occurred in relation to the rest of Scripture. This is just a general overview to help you place events in the Bible into their proper time and context. It will help as you study more passages to see how everything flows together. For extra context, you can use a Bible map book (or your study Bible) to note the location where the passage took place.

Day 2: Key Words and Verse Mapping
Take your memory verse (a key verse of your choice from your selected passage), and add it to the center box. Then, underline up to eight words that you want to explore further. In the smaller boxes, write one of the words you chose for each of them. Then, using a Bible app like Blue Letter Bible (available for free download on your phone), or a concordance, look up each of the words and write the key definitions. Often times Greek and Hebrew words were not able to be translated exactly word-for-word into English. So, this exercise will help you see more of the nuances in the original language. You can even use a regular dictionary in print or free online if you are not familiar with Bible apps or interlinear (Hebrew-Greek word) study. An example is provided for you on Day 2.

Day 3: Attributes of God & Worship
Today is a fun day! After your opening prayer, Bible memory review, and re-reading the passage, take some time to really look at the verses and note what you learn about God from them. Add the attributes you see into the boxes. (Some suggestions are available in the Appendix to get you started if you need help.) You may not use them all but really look for the subtle clues that God shows you about His character. Then, find the selected hymn or praise song online, or choose one of your own, and worship Him more fully keeping in mind all that He has shown you about Himself.

Instructions (continued):

Day 4: Cross-References & Translations

As you read the passage again today, choose another reputable Bible translation (not a paraphrase), and read it in that instead of your usual one. A translation (e.g., NIV, ESV, NASB, HCSB, KJV) differs from a paraphrase (e.g., The Message) in that they are done by a team of Biblical scholars and are written based on the original languages in a word-for-word or thought-for-thought style. Paraphrases are usually the work of one, or a few, individuals and often are based on the author's interpretation of Scripture. Some may include theological differences or biases that vary from the original manuscripts, and it is not always easy to recognize. It is an individual choice, but for the sake of this guide, I recommend you stay with trusted translations. (See Appendix for an overview of popular, reliable options.)

To get access to translations other than what you may have on hand, you can find them online by just searching the Scripture reference. Some trusted sites are Blue Letter Bible and Bible Hub. As you read, note the differences and similarities. Sometimes reading it in a slightly different version gives you new and deeper insight. As we noted on Day 2, the Hebrew and Greek languages often have several English words that fit appropriately. Here you will see the nuances of those languages in the chosen Scripture.

Then, using your key/memory verse and your own Bible, look in the margins for cross-references for that verse (or other verses that pique your interest). If you do not have them listed in your Bible, the above sites online are a good place to find cross-references for each verse.

Day 5: Commentaries & Life Application

Today is the day you tie everything together and learn how best to apply and live out what you learned from God's Word. Find some trusted commentaries (see Appendix for suggestions), and read about our week's passage. Make notes of any insights you learn. Then, pray and ask God how He wants you to apply what He has shown you.

Day 6: Review and Reflect

Today is just a day to go back over all that you did throughout the week and review your notes. Reflect on what God has shown you. Pray about it. Repent for any sins the Holy Spirit may have brought to mind. Consider again how you will live out the truths you learned throughout the week.

Day 7: Rest & Worship

God rested on the seventh day, and so should we. If you are doing this study on a Monday-Sunday, it should be Sunday today—so take some time to worship in a Bible-based church if you are able. Thank Him for all He has done. Praise Him again as you worship together with your brothers and sisters in Christ.

If you are doing this study and Day 7 falls on another day—take time to rest and worship, or follow another Bible reading plan of your choice.

God bless you as you seek Him each day!

Sample
Day One (M)
Context

<table>
<tr><td>1.</td><td>Pray</td></tr>
<tr><td>2.</td><td>Read passage</td></tr>
<tr><td>3.</td><td>Write memory verse</td></tr>
<tr><td>4.</td><td>Research context</td></tr>
<tr><td>5.</td><td>Add to timeline (p. 113)</td></tr>
<tr><td>6.</td><td>Pray</td></tr>
</table>

Prayer:

"Dear Lord, thank You for Your Holy Word. As I read and study this week about building on the rock, let me grow in my faith, and may You give it a sure and solid foundation on the Gospel of my Lord and Savior, Jesus Christ. In His Name. Amen."

Scripture Reading (Reference):

Matthew 7:24-29 (The house on the rock)

Bible Memory Verse:

Matthew 7:25—"And the rain fell, and the floods came, and the winds blew and slammed against that house; and yet it did not fall, for it had been founded on the rock."

Genre (circle one or more):

Historical/Narrative ~ Poetry/Wisdom ~ Prophecy/Apocalypse ~  Gospel ~ Epistle

Author:
Matthew (former tax collector who became one of Jesus's 12 disciples)
(Mark and Luke's Gospels refer to him as Levi, son of Alphaeus)

Audience:

Evangelistic to his fellow Jews, persuading them to recognize Jesus as their Messiah, encouragement to Jewish Christians to remain firm in their faith, and also reveals to Gentiles that the Gospel is available to them as well

Setting/Location:

Jesus is giving the Sermon on the Mount (Matthew chapters 5-7)
(thought to be on a hill near the northern shore of the Sea of Galilee near Capernaum)

Timeline (What was going on at the time?):
(Add to Bible Timeline p. 113)

After Jesus's baptism (Matthew 3), choosing His disciples (Matthew 4); probably around 31 B.C.

Day Two (T)
Key Words with Verse Mapping

1. Pray
2. Re-read passage
3. Review memory verse
4. Choose keywords from memory verse
5. Add one word to each box
6. Define w/ dictionary or interlinear (Hebrew-Greek)
7. Pray

Prayer:
"Dear Lord, thank You for this day. Please help me to glorify You in all I think, say, and do. Please draw all of my family and friends who don't know You to come and build their lives on the solid Rock, Jesus. Specifically I pray for _________________. In Jesus's Name. Amen."

Please note: adding lines to boxes is optional.

floods (potamos):
torrent, floods

house (oikia):
inhabited edifice, a dwelling; the inmates of a house, family; property, wealth, goods

founded (themelioo):
lay the foundation, make stable, establish

Bible Verse: Matthew 7:25

"And the rain fell, and the floods came, and the winds blew and slammed against that house; and yet it did not fall for it had been founded on the rock."

slammed against:
to fall forwards, fall down, to rush upon, beat against

rock (petra):
rock, large stone; metaphor for a man like a rock by reason of his firmness and strength of soul

fall (pipto):
to descend from a higher place to a lower, be thrust down, fall under judgment/condemnation; cast down from a state of prosperity or uprightness, perish, fall into ruin, lose authority/force, miss a share in something

Day Three (W)
Attributes of God
& Worship

1. Pray
2. Re-read passage
3. Review memory verse
4. Write what characteristics or attributes of God you see in the passage, and add one characteristic to each box
5. Choose a related hymn or worship song and spend time in worship and prayer.

Prayer:
"Dear Lord, please show me more of Yourself as I read Your Word today. Help me to know You better and love You more as I grow in my understanding of Who You are. Help me to worship You wholeheartedly, not just today but always.
In Jesus's Name, I pray. Amen."

Attributes of God:

authoritative	wise	loving
Provider	trustworthy	our sure, solid foundation
protective	all-powerful	trustworthy

Worship & Praise:

Hymn/Praise Song:

"My Hope is Built on Nothing Less"

Day Four (Th)
Cross-References
& Translations

1. Pray
2. Re-read passage in at least one other translation. Compare the readings.
3. Review memory verse
4. Look up cross-references and write the ones you choose into the boxes below.
5. Pray

Prayer:
"Dear Lord, as I read and study Your Word, please guide me into all Truth. Your Word is Truth. As I study the different translations of this passage, please show me all the details of meaning that You want to convey to my heart and mind. Help me to be discerning in all things. In Jesus's Name, I pray. Amen."

Cross-references:

Luke 6:47-49—wise person comes to Jesus, hears His words and does them—dug deep and laid the foundation on the rock
v.46—"Why do you call me Lord, Lord, and not do what I tell you?"

Matthew 25:1-13—5 foolish and 5 wise virgins

Ezekiel 13:10-14—false prophets condemned, people were only "white-washing their walls", no substance, will fall with rain, hailstones, and wind of God's wrath

1 Corinthians 3:14—"If any man's work which he has built on it remains, he will receive a reward."

1 Peter 1:7—"so that the proof of your faith, being more precious than gold which is perishable, even though tested by fire, may be found to result in praise and glory and honor at the revelation of Jesus Christ;"

Day Five (F)
Commentaries & Life Application

1.	Pray
2.	Re-read passage
3.	Review memory verse
4.	Research commentaries
5.	Write out how you will apply what God has shown you in your reading
6.	Pray

Prayer:

"Dear Lord, please help me and my family to build our lives on the solid Rock, Jesus Christ. May all our hopes, plans, and dreams be found in Him. May our lives reflect our love for Him as demonstrated by our obedience. In Jesus's Name. Amen."

Commentary Insights:

Matthew Henry (Blue Letter Bible app):

- chapter shows indispensable necessity of obeying Christ
- Shows that an outward profession of religion, no matter how impressive, will not bring us to heaven unless accompanied by true faith and heart-felt obedience
- Christ separates the doers from the merely hearers who don't put into practice what He says
- We are blessed when we obey Jesus's commands
- Actually doing and living out God's Word is what builds our lives on a solid foundation that will bring blessing and stability no matter what storms may come
- Building on anything other than Jesus will certainly fail when storms/temptations/persecution comes.
- Reference to Mary and Martha—where Mary chose the "good portion", listening to Jesus rather than just going about working for Him without paying attention to and giving Him our devotion

How do I live out what I learned?

- Evidence of true faith is obedience to what Jesus said.
- Building our lives on Jesus is truly wise; the only sure foundation in a culture that is continually shifting or changing. God's values and His Word stand firm against the test of time.
- Building a strong foundation requires going deep into the bedrock—just as we need to go deep into God's Word, prayer, and our relationship with Him.
- "Surface righteousness" has no root or foundation and won't stand up under trials, hardship, or persecution.
- PRAY for help to live out what I learned.
- REPENT of my attempts to merely perform my "religious duties" rather than digging deep and obeying from a pure heart.
- Spend daily time in His Word and prayer. Continue to study and learn His Word, so I can better live it out.
- Memorize more Scripture (hide it in my heart) so I can obey and live according to His eternal truths.

Sample
Day Six (Sa):
Review & Reflect

Day Seven (Su):
Rest & Worship

1.	Pray
2.	Re-read passage
3.	Review memory verse (Can you recite by memory?)
4.	Review previous days' content
5.	Reflection questions
6.	Pray

Prayer:

"Dear Lord, thank You for giving me this time in Your Word this week to grow in my knowledge of You. Thank You for helping me to build my life more firmly on the Rock of my salvation. Now I ask that You would let me rest in Your truths and worship You fully today and every day. In Jesus's Precious and Holy Name. Amen."

Reflection Questions:

1.) What was the biggest takeaway or key point that God impressed on you this week?

I need to spend time with God daily and dig deep into His Word to learn and live out His truths. Mere outward religious duties are superficial and will not stand up under hardship or persecution if my heart is not changed by Him and my faith is not securely placed in Jesus, my Rock, and my Redeemer.

2.) What did you learn about God from this passage?

He is the Creator of all—me, nature, etc. He is my only sure hope in an ever-changing world. He wants us to love Him, have faith in Him, and build our lives on the solid foundation of His Word. He is my Protector and Provider. I can trust Him and rely on the truth of His Word and promises no matter what this world tries to throw our way.

3.) What did you learn about yourself? Are there any areas you need to repent of or change?

(answers will vary)

4.) What action steps can I take to better live out what God has taught me through His Word?

(answers will vary)

5.) Other thoughts:

(answers will vary)

Day One (M)
Context

1. Pray
2. Read passage
3. Write memory verse
4. Research context
5. Add to timeline (p. 113)
6. Pray

Prayer:

Scripture Reading (Reference):

Bible Memory Verse:

Genre (circle one or more):

Historical/Narrative ~ Poetry/Wisdom ~ Prophecy/Apocalypse ~ Gospel ~ Epistle

Author:

Audience:

Setting/Location:

Timeline (What was going on at the time?):
(Add to Bible Timeline p. 113)

Day Two (T)
Key Words with Verse Mapping

1. Pray
2. Re-read passage
3. Review memory verse
4. Choose keywords from memory verse
5. Add one word to each box
6. Define w/ dictionary or interlinear (Hebrew-Greek)
7. Pray

Prayer:

Bible Verse:

Day Three (W)
Attributes of God
& Worship

1. Pray
2. Re-read passage
3. Review memory verse
4. Write what characteristics or attributes of God you see in the passage, and add one characteristic to each box
5. Choose a related hymn or worship song and spend time in worship and prayer.

Prayer:

Attributes of God:

Worship & Praise:

Hymn/Praise Song:

Day Four (Th)
Cross-References
& Translations

1. Pray
2. Re-read passage in at least one other translation. Compare the readings.
3. Review memory verse
4. Look up cross-references and write the ones you choose into the boxes below.
5. Pray

Prayer:

Cross-references:

Day Five (F)
Commentaries &
Life Application

1. Pray
2. Re-read passage
3. Review memory verse
4. Research commentaries
5. Write out how you will apply what God has shown you in your reading
6. Pray

Prayer:

Commentary Insights:

How do I live out what I learned?

Day Six (Sa):
Review & Reflect

Day Seven (Su):
Rest & Worship

1. Pray
2. Re-read passage
3. Review memory verse
   (Can you recite by memory?)
4. Review previous days' content
5. Reflection questions
6. Pray

Prayer:

Reflection Questions:

1.) What was the biggest takeaway or key point that God impressed on you this week?

2.) What did you learn about God from this passage?

3.) What did you learn about yourself? Are there any areas you need to repent of or change?

4.) What action steps can I take to better live out what God has taught me through His Word?

5.) Other thoughts:

Notes

Notes

Day One (M)
Context

1. Pray
2. Read passage
3. Write memory verse
4. Research context
5. Add to timeline (p. 113)
6. Pray

Prayer:

Scripture Reading (Reference):

Bible Memory Verse:

Genre (circle one or more):

Historical/Narrative ~ Poetry/Wisdom ~ Prophecy/Apocalypse ~ Gospel ~ Epistle

Author:

Audience:

Setting/Location:

Timeline (What was going on at the time?):
(Add to Bible Timeline p. 113)

Day Two (T)
Key Words with Verse Mapping

1. Pray
2. Re-read passage
3. Review memory verse
4. Choose keywords from memory verse
5. Add one word to each box
6. Define w/ dictionary or interlinear (Hebrew-Greek)
7. Pray

Prayer:

Bible Verse:

Day Three (W)
Attributes of God & Worship

1. Pray
2. Re-read passage
3. Review memory verse
4. Write what characteristics or attributes of God you see in the passage, and add one characteristic to each box
5. Choose a related hymn or worship song and spend time in worship and prayer.

Prayer:

Attributes of God:

Worship & Praise:

Hymn/Praise Song:

Day Four (Th)
Cross-References
& Translations

1. Pray
2. Re-read passage in at least one other translation. Compare the readings.
3. Review memory verse
4. Look up cross-references and write the ones you choose into the boxes below.
5. Pray

Prayer:

Cross-references:

Day Five (F)
Commentaries & Life Application

1.	Pray
2.	Re-read passage
3.	Review memory verse
4.	Research commentaries
5.	Write out how you will apply what God has shown you in your reading
6.	Pray

Prayer:

Commentary Insights:

How do I live out what I learned?

Day Six (Sa):
Review & Reflect

Day Seven (Su):
Rest & Worship

1. Pray
2. Re-read passage
3. Review memory verse
   (Can you recite by memory?)
4. Review previous days' content
5. Reflection questions
6. Pray

Prayer:

Reflection Questions:

1.) What was the biggest takeaway or key point that God impressed on you this week?

2.) What did you learn about God from this passage?

3.) What did you learn about yourself? Are there any areas you need to repent of or change?

4.) What action steps can I take to better live out what God has taught me through His Word?

5.) Other thoughts:

Notes

Notes

Day One (M)
Context

<table>
<tr><td>1.</td><td>Pray</td></tr>
<tr><td>2.</td><td>Read passage</td></tr>
<tr><td>3.</td><td>Write memory verse</td></tr>
<tr><td>4.</td><td>Research context</td></tr>
<tr><td>5.</td><td>Add to timeline (p. 113)</td></tr>
<tr><td>6.</td><td>Pray</td></tr>
</table>

Prayer:

Scripture Reading (Reference):

Bible Memory Verse:

Genre (circle one or more):

Historical/Narrative ~ Poetry/Wisdom ~ Prophecy/Apocalypse ~ Gospel ~ Epistle

Author:

Audience:

Setting/Location:

Timeline (What was going on at the time?):
(Add to Bible Timeline p. 113)

Day Two (T)
Key Words with
Verse Mapping

1. Pray
2. Re-read passage
3. Review memory verse
4. Choose keywords from memory verse
5. Add one word to each box
6. Define w/ dictionary or interlinear (Hebrew-Greek)
7. Pray

Prayer:

Bible Verse:

Day Three (W)
Attributes of God & Worship

1. Pray
2. Re-read passage
3. Review memory verse
4. Write what characteristics or attributes of God you see in the passage, and add one characteristic to each box
5. Choose a related hymn or worship song and spend time in worship and prayer.

Prayer:

Attributes of God:

Worship & Praise:

Hymn/Praise Song:

Day Four (Th)
Cross-References
& Translations

1. Pray
2. Re-read passage in at least one other translation. Compare the readings.
3. Review memory verse
4. Look up cross-references and write the ones you choose into the boxes below.
5. Pray

Prayer:

Cross-references:

Day Five (F)
Commentaries &
Life Application

1. Pray
2. Re-read passage
3. Review memory verse
4. Research commentaries
5. Write out how you will apply what God has shown you in your reading
6. Pray

Prayer:

Commentary Insights:

How do I live out what I learned?

Day Six (Sa):
Review & Reflect

Day Seven (Su):
Rest & Worship

1. Pray
2. Re-read passage
3. Review memory verse
   (Can you recite by memory?)
4. Review previous days' content
5. Reflection questions
6. Pray

Prayer:

Reflection Questions:

1.) What was the biggest takeaway or key point that God impressed on you this week?

2.) What did you learn about God from this passage?

3.) What did you learn about yourself? Are there any areas you need to repent of or change?

4.) What action steps can I take to better live out what God has taught me through His Word?

5.) Other thoughts:

Notes

Notes

Day One (M)
Context

1. Pray
2. Read passage
3. Write memory verse
4. Research context
5. Add to timeline (p. 113)
6. Pray

Prayer:

Scripture Reading (Reference):

Bible Memory Verse:

Genre (circle one or more):

Historical/Narrative ~ Poetry/Wisdom ~ Prophecy/Apocalypse ~ Gospel ~ Epistle

Author:

Audience:

Setting/Location:

Timeline (What was going on at the time?):
(Add to Bible Timeline p. 113)

Day Two (T)
Key Words with Verse Mapping

1. Pray
2. Re-read passage
3. Review memory verse
4. Choose keywords from memory verse
5. Add one word to each box
6. Define w/ dictionary or interlinear (Hebrew-Greek)
7. Pray

Prayer:

Bible Verse:

Day Three (W)
Attributes of God & Worship

1. Pray
2. Re-read passage
3. Review memory verse
4. Write what characteristics or attributes of God you see in the passage, and add one characteristic to each box
5. Choose a related hymn or worship song and spend time in worship and prayer.

Prayer:

Attributes of God:

Worship & Praise:

Hymn/Praise Song:

Day Four (Th)
Cross-References & Translations

1. Pray
2. Re-read passage in at least one other translation. Compare the readings.
3. Review memory verse
4. Look up cross-references and write the ones you choose into the boxes below.
5. Pray

Prayer:

Cross-references:

Day Five (F)
Commentaries &
Life Application

1. Pray
2. Re-read passage
3. Review memory verse
4. Research commentaries
5. Write out how you will apply what God has shown you in your reading
6. Pray

Prayer:

Commentary Insights:

How do I live out what I learned?

Day Six (Sa):
Review & Reflect

Day Seven (Su):
Rest & Worship

1. Pray
2. Re-read passage
3. Review memory verse
   (Can you recite by memory?)
4. Review previous days' content
5. Reflection questions
6. Pray

Prayer:

Reflection Questions:

1.) What was the biggest takeaway or key point that God impressed on you this week?

2.) What did you learn about God from this passage?

3.) What did you learn about yourself? Are there any areas you need to repent of or change?

4.) What action steps can I take to better live out what God has taught me through His Word?

5.) Other thoughts:

Notes

Notes

1. Pray
2. Read passage
3. Write memory verse
4. Research context
5. Add to timeline (p. 113)
6. Pray

Prayer:

Scripture Reading (Reference):

Bible Memory Verse:

Genre (circle one or more):

Historical/Narrative ~ Poetry/Wisdom ~ Prophecy/Apocalypse ~ Gospel ~ Epistle

Author:

Audience:

Setting/Location:

Timeline (What was going on at the time?):
(Add to Bible Timeline p. 113)

Day Two (T)
Key Words with Verse Mapping

1. Pray
2. Re-read passage
3. Review memory verse
4. Choose keywords from memory verse
5. Add one word to each box
6. Define w/ dictionary or interlinear (Hebrew-Greek)
7. Pray

Prayer:

Bible Verse:

Day Three (W)
Attributes of God & Worship

1. Pray
2. Re-read passage
3. Review memory verse
4. Write what characteristics or attributes of God you see in the passage, and add one characteristic to each box
5. Choose a related hymn or worship song and spend time in worship and prayer.

Prayer:

Attributes of God:

Worship & Praise:

Hymn/Praise Song:

Day Four (Th)
Cross-References
& Translations

1. Pray
2. Re-read passage in at least one other translation. Compare the readings.
3. Review memory verse
4. Look up cross-references and write the ones you choose into the boxes below.
5. Pray

Prayer:

Cross-references:

Day Five (F)
Commentaries &
Life Application

1. Pray
2. Re-read passage
3. Review memory verse
4. Research commentaries
5. Write out how you will apply what God has shown you in your reading
6. Pray

Prayer:

Commentary Insights:

How do I live out what I learned?

Day Six (Sa):
Review & Reflect

Day Seven (Su):
Rest & Worship

1. Pray
2. Re-read passage
3. Review memory verse
   (Can you recite by memory?)
4. Review previous days' content
5. Reflection questions
6. Pray

Prayer:

Reflection Questions:

1.) What was the biggest takeaway or key point that God impressed on you this week?

2.) What did you learn about God from this passage?

3.) What did you learn about yourself? Are there any areas you need to repent of or change?

4.) What action steps can I take to better live out what God has taught me through His Word?

5.) Other thoughts:

Notes

Notes

Day One (M)
Context

1.   Pray
2.   Read passage
3.   Write memory verse
4.   Research context
5.   Add to timeline (p. 113)
6.   Pray

Prayer:

Scripture Reading (Reference):

Bible Memory Verse:

Genre (circle one or more):

Historical/Narrative ~ Poetry/Wisdom ~ Prophecy/Apocalypse ~ Gospel ~ Epistle

Author:

Audience:

Setting/Location:

Timeline (What was going on at the time?):
(Add to Bible Timeline p. 113)

Day Two (T)
Key Words with Verse Mapping

1. Pray
2. Re-read passage
3. Review memory verse
4. Choose keywords from memory verse
5. Add one word to each box
6. Define w/ dictionary or interlinear (Hebrew-Greek)
7. Pray

Prayer:

Bible Verse:

Day Three (W)
Attributes of God & Worship

1. Pray
2. Re-read passage
3. Review memory verse
4. Write what characteristics or attributes of God you see in the passage, and add one characteristic to each box
5. Choose a related hymn or worship song and spend time in worship and prayer.

Prayer:

Attributes of God:

Worship & Praise:

Hymn/Praise Song:

Day Four (Th)
Cross-References
& Translations

1. Pray
2. Re-read passage in at least one other translation. Compare the readings.
3. Review memory verse
4. Look up cross-references and write the ones you choose into the boxes below.
5. Pray

Prayer:

Cross-references:

Day Five (F)
Commentaries &
Life Application

1. Pray
2. Re-read passage
3. Review memory verse
4. Research commentaries
5. Write out how you will apply what God has shown you in your reading
6. Pray

Prayer:

Commentary Insights:

How do I live out what I learned?

Day Six (Sa):
Review & Reflect

Day Seven (Su):
Rest & Worship

1. Pray
2. Re-read passage
3. Review memory verse
   (Can you recite by memory?)
4. Review previous days' content
5. Reflection questions
6. Pray

Prayer:

Reflection Questions:

1.) What was the biggest takeaway or key point that God impressed on you this week?

2.) What did you learn about God from this passage?

3.) What did you learn about yourself? Are there any areas you need to repent of or change?

4.) What action steps can I take to better live out what God has taught me through His Word?

5.) Other thoughts:

Notes

Notes

Day One (M)
Context

<table>
<tr><td>1.</td><td>Pray</td></tr>
<tr><td>2.</td><td>Read passage</td></tr>
<tr><td>3.</td><td>Write memory verse</td></tr>
<tr><td>4.</td><td>Research context</td></tr>
<tr><td>5.</td><td>Add to timeline (p. 113)</td></tr>
<tr><td>6.</td><td>Pray</td></tr>
</table>

Prayer:

Scripture Reading (Reference):

Bible Memory Verse:

Genre (circle one or more):

Historical/Narrative ~ Poetry/Wisdom ~ Prophecy/Apocalypse ~ Gospel ~ Epistle

Author:

Audience:

Setting/Location:

Timeline (What was going on at the time?):
(Add to Bible Timeline p. 113)

Day Two (T)
Key Words with Verse Mapping

1. Pray
2. Re-read passage
3. Review memory verse
4. Choose keywords from memory verse
5. Add one word to each box
6. Define w/ dictionary or interlinear (Hebrew-Greek)
7. Pray

Prayer:

Bible Verse:

Day Three (W)
Attributes of God & Worship

1. Pray
2. Re-read passage
3. Review memory verse
4. Write what characteristics or attributes of God you see in the passage, and add one characteristic to each box
5. Choose a related hymn or worship song and spend time in worship and prayer.

Prayer:

Attributes of God:

Worship & Praise:

Hymn/Praise Song:

Day Four (Th)
Cross-References
& Translations

1. Pray
2. Re-read passage in at least one other translation. Compare the readings.
3. Review memory verse
4. Look up cross-references and write the ones you choose into the boxes below.
5. Pray

Prayer:

Cross-references:

Day Five (F)
Commentaries &
Life Application

1. Pray
2. Re-read passage
3. Review memory verse
4. Research commentaries
5. Write out how you will apply what God has shown you in your reading
6. Pray

Prayer:

Commentary Insights:

How do I live out what I learned?

Day Six (Sa):
Review & Reflect

Day Seven (Su):
Rest & Worship

1. Pray
2. Re-read passage
3. Review memory verse
   (Can you recite by memory?)
4. Review previous days' content
5. Reflection questions
6. Pray

Prayer:

Reflection Questions:

1.) What was the biggest takeaway or key point that God impressed on you this week?

2.) What did you learn about God from this passage?

3.) What did you learn about yourself? Are there any areas you need to repent of or change?

4.) What action steps can I take to better live out what God has taught me through His Word?

5.) Other thoughts:

Notes

Notes

Day One (M)
Context

1.   Pray
2.   Read passage
3.   Write memory verse
4.   Research context
5.   Add to timeline (p. 113)
6.   Pray

Prayer:

Scripture Reading (Reference):

Bible Memory Verse:

Genre (circle one or more):

Historical/Narrative ~ Poetry/Wisdom ~ Prophecy/Apocalypse ~ Gospel ~ Epistle

Author:

Audience:

Setting/Location:

Timeline (What was going on at the time?):
(Add to Bible Timeline p. 113)

Day Two (T)
Key Words with Verse Mapping

1. Pray
2. Re-read passage
3. Review memory verse
4. Choose keywords from memory verse
5. Add one word to each box
6. Define w/ dictionary or interlinear (Hebrew-Greek)
7. Pray

Prayer:

Bible Verse:

Day Three (W)
Attributes of God & Worship

1. Pray
2. Re-read passage
3. Review memory verse
4. Write what characteristics or attributes of God you see in the passage, and add one characteristic to each box
5. Choose a related hymn or worship song and spend time in worship and prayer.

Prayer:

Attributes of God:

Worship & Praise:

Hymn/Praise Song:

Day Four (Th)
Cross-References
& Translations

1. Pray
2. Re-read passage in at least one other translation. Compare the readings.
3. Review memory verse
4. Look up cross-references and write the ones you choose into the boxes below.
5. Pray

Prayer:

Cross-references:

Day Five (F)
Commentaries & Life Application

1. Pray
2. Re-read passage
3. Review memory verse
4. Research commentaries
5. Write out how you will apply what God has shown you in your reading
6. Pray

Prayer:

Commentary Insights:

How do I live out what I learned?

Day Six (Sa):
Review & Reflect

Day Seven (Su):
Rest & Worship

1. Pray
2. Re-read passage
3. Review memory verse
   (Can you recite by memory?)
4. Review previous days' content
5. Reflection questions
6. Pray

Prayer:

Reflection Questions:

1.) What was the biggest takeaway or key point that God impressed on you this week?

2.) What did you learn about God from this passage?

3.) What did you learn about yourself? Are there any areas you need to repent of or change?

4.) What action steps can I take to better live out what God has taught me through His Word?

5.) Other thoughts:

Notes

Notes

Day One (M)
Context

<table>
<tr><td>1.</td><td>Pray</td></tr>
<tr><td>2.</td><td>Read passage</td></tr>
<tr><td>3.</td><td>Write memory verse</td></tr>
<tr><td>4.</td><td>Research context</td></tr>
<tr><td>5.</td><td>Add to timeline (p. 113)</td></tr>
<tr><td>6.</td><td>Pray</td></tr>
</table>

Prayer:

Scripture Reading (Reference):

Bible Memory Verse:

Genre (circle one or more):

Historical/Narrative ~ Poetry/Wisdom ~ Prophecy/Apocalypse ~ Gospel ~ Epistle

Author:

Audience:

Setting/Location:

Timeline (What was going on at the time?):
(Add to Bible Timeline p. 113)

Day Two (T)
Key Words with Verse Mapping

1. Pray
2. Re-read passage
3. Review memory verse
4. Choose keywords from memory verse
5. Add one word to each box
6. Define w/ dictionary or interlinear (Hebrew-Greek)
7. Pray

Prayer:

Bible Verse:

Day Three (W)
Attributes of God
& Worship

1. Pray
2. Re-read passage
3. Review memory verse
4. Write what characteristics or attributes of God you see in the passage, and add one characteristic to each box
5. Choose a related hymn or worship song and spend time in worship and prayer.

Prayer:

Attributes of God:

Worship & Praise:

Hymn/Praise Song:

Day Four (Th)
Cross-References
& Translations

1. Pray
2. Re-read passage in at least one other translation. Compare the readings.
3. Review memory verse
4. Look up cross-references and write the ones you choose into the boxes below.
5. Pray

Prayer:

Cross-references:

Day Five (F)
Commentaries &
Life Application

1. Pray
2. Re-read passage
3. Review memory verse
4. Research commentaries
5. Write out how you will apply what God has shown you in your reading
6. Pray

Prayer:

Commentary Insights:

How do I live out what I learned?

Day Six (Sa):
Review & Reflect

Day Seven (Su):
Rest & Worship

1. Pray
2. Re-read passage
3. Review memory verse
   (Can you recite by memory?)
4. Review previous days' content
5. Reflection questions
6. Pray

Prayer:

Reflection Questions:

1.) What was the biggest takeaway or key point that God impressed on you this week?

2.) What did you learn about God from this passage?

3.) What did you learn about yourself? Are there any areas you need to repent of or change?

4.) What action steps can I take to better live out what God has taught me through His Word?

5.) Other thoughts:

Notes

Notes

Day One (M)
Context

1.   Pray
2.   Read passage
3.   Write memory verse
4.   Research context
5.   Add to timeline (p. 113)
6.   Pray

Prayer:

Scripture Reading (Reference):

Bible Memory Verse:

Genre (circle one or more):

Historical/Narrative ~ Poetry/Wisdom ~ Prophecy/Apocalypse ~ Gospel ~ Epistle

Author:

Audience:

Setting/Location:

Timeline (What was going on at the time?):
(Add to Bible Timeline p. 113)

Day Two (T)
Key Words with Verse Mapping

1. Pray
2. Re-read passage
3. Review memory verse
4. Choose keywords from memory verse
5. Add one word to each box
6. Define w/ dictionary or interlinear (Hebrew-Greek)
7. Pray

Prayer:

Bible Verse:

Day Three (W)
Attributes of God & Worship

1. Pray
2. Re-read passage
3. Review memory verse
4. Write what characteristics or attributes of God you see in the passage, and add one characteristic to each box
5. Choose a related hymn or worship song and spend time in worship and prayer.

Prayer:

Attributes of God:

Worship & Praise:

Hymn/Praise Song:

Day Four (Th)
Cross-References
& Translations

1. Pray
2. Re-read passage in at least one other translation. Compare the readings.
3. Review memory verse
4. Look up cross-references and write the ones you choose into the boxes below.
5. Pray

Prayer:

Cross-references:

Day Five (F)
Commentaries &
Life Application

1. Pray
2. Re-read passage
3. Review memory verse
4. Research commentaries
5. Write out how you will apply what God has shown you in your reading
6. Pray

Prayer:

Commentary Insights:

How do I live out what I learned?

Day Six (Sa):
Review & Reflect

Day Seven (Su):
Rest & Worship

1. Pray
2. Re-read passage
3. Review memory verse
   (Can you recite by memory?)
4. Review previous days' content
5. Reflection questions
6. Pray

Prayer:

Reflection Questions:

1.) What was the biggest takeaway or key point that God impressed on you this week?

2.) What did you learn about God from this passage?

3.) What did you learn about yourself? Are there any areas you need to repent of or change?

4.) What action steps can I take to better live out what God has taught me through His Word?

5.) Other thoughts:

Notes

Notes

Day One (M)
Context

<table>
<tr><td>1.</td><td>Pray</td></tr>
<tr><td>2.</td><td>Read passage</td></tr>
<tr><td>3.</td><td>Write memory verse</td></tr>
<tr><td>4.</td><td>Research context</td></tr>
<tr><td>5.</td><td>Add to timeline (p. 113)</td></tr>
<tr><td>6.</td><td>Pray</td></tr>
</table>

Prayer:

Scripture Reading (Reference):

Bible Memory Verse:

Genre (circle one or more):

Historical/Narrative ~ Poetry/Wisdom ~ Prophecy/Apocalypse ~ Gospel ~ Epistle

Author:

Audience:

Setting/Location:

Timeline (What was going on at the time?):
(Add to Bible Timeline p. 113)

Day Two (T)
Key Words with
Verse Mapping

1. Pray
2. Re-read passage
3. Review memory verse
4. Choose keywords from memory verse
5. Add one word to each box
6. Define w/ dictionary or interlinear (Hebrew-Greek)
7. Pray

Prayer:

Bible Verse:

Day Three (W)
Attributes of God & Worship

1. Pray
2. Re-read passage
3. Review memory verse
4. Write what characteristics or attributes of God you see in the passage, and add one characteristic to each box
5. Choose a related hymn or worship song and spend time in worship and prayer.

Prayer:

Attributes of God:

Worship & Praise:

Hymn/Praise Song:

Day Four (Th)
Cross-References
& Translations

1. Pray
2. Re-read passage in at least one other translation. Compare the readings.
3. Review memory verse
4. Look up cross-references and write the ones you choose into the boxes below.
5. Pray

Prayer:

Cross-references:

Day Five (F)
Commentaries &
Life Application

1.	Pray
2.	Re-read passage
3.	Review memory verse
4.	Research commentaries
5.	Write out how you will apply what God has shown you in your reading
6.	Pray

Prayer:

Commentary Insights:

How do I live out what I learned?

Day Six (Sa):
Review & Reflect

Day Seven (Su):
Rest & Worship

1. Pray
2. Re-read passage
3. Review memory verse
   (Can you recite by memory?)
4. Review previous days' content
5. Reflection questions
6. Pray

Prayer:

Reflection Questions:

1.) What was the biggest takeaway or key point that God impressed on you this week?

2.) What did you learn about God from this passage?

3.) What did you learn about yourself? Are there any areas you need to repent of or change?

4.) What action steps can I take to better live out what God has taught me through His Word?

5.) Other thoughts:

Notes

Notes

Day One (M)
Context

1.   Pray
2.   Read passage
3.   Write memory verse
4.   Research context
5.   Add to timeline (p. 113)
6.   Pray

Prayer:

Scripture Reading (Reference):

Bible Memory Verse:

Genre (circle one or more):

  Historical/Narrative ~ Poetry/Wisdom ~ Prophecy/Apocalypse ~ Gospel ~ Epistle

Author:

Audience:

Setting/Location:

Timeline (What was going on at the time?):
(Add to Bible Timeline p. 113)

Day Two (T)
Key Words with Verse Mapping

1. Pray
2. Re-read passage
3. Review memory verse
4. Choose keywords from memory verse
5. Add one word to each box
6. Define w/ dictionary or interlinear (Hebrew-Greek)
7. Pray

Prayer:

Bible Verse:

Day Three (W)
Attributes of God
& Worship

1. Pray
2. Re-read passage
3. Review memory verse
4. Write what characteristics or attributes of God you see in the passage, and add one characteristic to each box
5. Choose a related hymn or worship song and spend time in worship and prayer.

Prayer:

Attributes of God:

Worship & Praise:

Hymn/Praise Song:

Day Four (Th)
Cross-References
& Translations

1. Pray
2. Re-read passage in at least one other translation. Compare the readings.
3. Review memory verse
4. Look up cross-references and write the ones you choose into the boxes below.
5. Pray

Prayer:

Cross-references:

Day Five (F)
Commentaries & Life Application

1. Pray
2. Re-read passage
3. Review memory verse
4. Research commentaries
5. Write out how you will apply what God has shown you in your reading
6. Pray

Prayer:

Commentary Insights:

How do I live out what I learned?

Day Six (Sa):
Review & Reflect

Day Seven (Su):
Rest & Worship

1. Pray
2. Re-read passage
3. Review memory verse
   (Can you recite by memory?)
4. Review previous days' content
5. Reflection questions
6. Pray

Prayer:

Reflection Questions:

1.) What was the biggest takeaway or key point that God impressed on you this week?

2.) What did you learn about God from this passage?

3.) What did you learn about yourself? Are there any areas you need to repent of or change?

4.) What action steps can I take to better live out what God has taught me through His Word?

5.) Other thoughts:

Notes

Notes

Appendix

Attributes of God (examples):

- All-powerful (omnipotent)
- All-knowing (omniscient)
- All-present (omnipresent)
- Authoritative
- Awesome
- Compassionate
- Creator
- Eternal
- Faithful
- Forgiving
- Glorious
- Good
- Gracious
- Holy
- Infinite (no beginning or end)
- Jealous (for His people)
- Just
- Kind
- Loving
- Merciful
- Patient
- Perfect
- Praise-worthy
- Protective
- Provider
- Righteous
- Self-existent (needs nothing else to exist)
- Sovereign (in complete control)
- Trustworthy
- Truthful
- Unchanging (immutable)
- Wise
- Wonderful

Trusted Commentaries and Study Bibles with Notes:

*Please note that these are just suggestions from generally reliable Bible teachers and authors. This does not mean that this author agrees with everything stated in their writings, but as a rule, they are trustworthy sources of Biblical insights and information. Many are available online for free, or in e-book versions for very low cost. You may want to invest in a few of these resources if you haven't already because they will provide a lifetime of enrichment to your Bible study time. You can also access many of these from free online or downloadable programs such as Blue Letter Bible (www.blueletterbible.org) or E-Sword (www.e-sword.net)

- ESV Study Bible
- The ESV Reformation Study Bible (Edited by: R.C. Sproul of Ligonier Ministries)
- ESV Expository Commentaries (by: Crossway Books)
- KJV Reformation Heritage Study Bible
- Matthew Henry Commentaries (available in print or in Blue Letter Bible online/app)
- Charles Spurgeon Commentaries (available in print or in Blue Letter Bible online/app)
- Martin Luther Commentaries
- Life Application New Testament Commentary
- Strong's Exhaustive Concordance of the Bible
- Ligonier.org (commentaries, sermons, and resources for every book of the Bible)

Bibles Translation Overview:

*Please note that this is just a general overview of some major, trusted Bible translations available today.

- King James Version (KJV): translated in 1611, uses old English language that may be difficult for modern readers, but it is a faithful word-for-word translation. Word-for-word translations mean that each original language term is translated as best as possible into an equivalent English word. This can sometimes lead to awkward phrasing, as there are not always exact English replications of every term found in the original texts.

- New American Standard Bible (1995 ed.): considered the most accurate word-for-word version in the English language; recent updates have been issued, but the 1995 edition is considered standard.

- English Standard Version (ESV): very popular, word-for-word modern translation used in many churches today.

- Holman Christian Standard Bible (HCSB): modern, easy-to-read translation that is balanced between word-for-word and thought-for-thought

- New International Version (NIV): popular, modern, thought-for-thought translation that is easy to read and understand. Thought-for-thought translations are more interpretive than word-for-word versions, as the translators' goal is to share the original meaning of the text rather than translate each word as found in the original manuscripts. The NIV was used in churches frequently in the past few decades but has slowly been replaced by the ESV in many places.

- New Living Translation (NLT): modern, very easy-to-read thought-for-thought translation that is close to a paraphrase. This version can be helpful when trying to understand more difficult passages or explain concepts to newer believers or seekers.

Bible Book Genres Overview:

The Bible is one large book that is actually comprised of 66 smaller books. Each one tells a unified story that ultimately points to our Lord and Savior Jesus Christ.

Each of those smaller books usually falls into one or more general genres, or types, of literature. Knowing the genre of the book you are reading will help you more accurately interpret and apply God's Word.

As noted on Day 1 of this guide, you are asked to circle one (or more, if applicable) of the major genres for the selection you are reading for the week. Here is a brief overview of those categories, and many of the Bible books that each usually falls into, in case you are having any difficulty deciding what to choose for your particular passage. Some sources may have slightly different categories, but this will give you a good place to start.

- **Historical/Narrative**—These books generally tell the story of what happened in history or detail specific events. Technically, most Bible books have aspects that are historical. But for our purposes, this section includes the Law books like Leviticus and Deuteronomy where God details His plans for government and worship for the nation of Israel. It also includes historical books like Genesis, Exodus, Numbers, Joshua, Judges, 1 and 2 Samuel, 1 and 2 Kings, 1 and 2 Chronicles, Ezra, Nehemiah, and Acts.

- **Poetry/Wisdom**—These books are generally in poetic form and contain insights for daily living based on a Biblical worldview. Examples include the Psalms, Proverbs, Job, Ecclesiastes, Lamentations, and Song of Solomon (or Song of Songs).

- **Prophecy/Apocalypse**—This includes the four major prophets (Isaiah, Jeremiah, Ezekiel, Daniel) and the 12 minor prophets (Hosea through Malachi). God sent His prophets to warn the nation of Israel and call them to repent when they turned away from Him. Apocalyptic books include Revelation and parts of the book of Daniel. They are often very symbolic in their imagery and usually predict future events from the time of writing.

- **Gospels**— The four Gospels (Matthew, Mark, Luke, and John) detail the life and works of Jesus Christ, including His most important work—saving us through His death on the cross and resurrection from the dead. Through this work, He has covered all our sins and restored us to a right relationship with God our Father when we repent and put our trust in Him alone.

- **Epistles**—The epistles (or letters) include a majority of the New Testament content found after the Gospels. Many are written by the Apostle Paul (and others by their namesakes), as letters to the early Christian churches throughout the world at that time. They include some theological doctrine as well as principles for Christian living. But context and the original audience must always be taken into consideration to arrive at the correct interpretation and application of the Word.

Recommended Resources and More Information:

See thebiblebasedlife.com for recommended prayer books, study Bibles, Bible study tools, and more resources to help enhance your daily quiet time.
You can also sign up for updates and get free Bible studies and devotionals!

If you purchased this book as a print copy, would you please leave a review to let others know how this journal might help them grow in the Word? We can all work together to spread the good news of the Gospel of our Lord and Savior, Jesus Christ! Thank you very much!!

About the Author:

Heather Erdmann is a Christian wife, mom, dental hygienist, devotional writer for Lifeway, and best-selling author of "Why the Bible Makes Life Make Sense: Pursuing a Purposeful Life with a Biblical Perspective," "Unlocking the Mystery of Marriage: Loving Your Spouse the Way Christ Loves the Church." She loves helping busy Christian women focus on Jesus, understand the Bible, and ultimately fall more in love with the Author Himself.

Her experience includes online training from Southeastern Baptist Theological Seminary and the Biblical Counseling Institute. For over 30 years she has written devotions and Bible studies for women, taught children's Sunday School and Vacation Bible school, and participated in homeschool curriculum development. She also plays flute and oboe for her local church worship team.

When not working or writing, she loves drinking coffee with friends, studying the Bible, cuddling (or napping with) her kitties, taking day trips with her family, or camping with her husband.

Bible Timeline Overview
(Dates are approximate)

OLD TESTAMENT

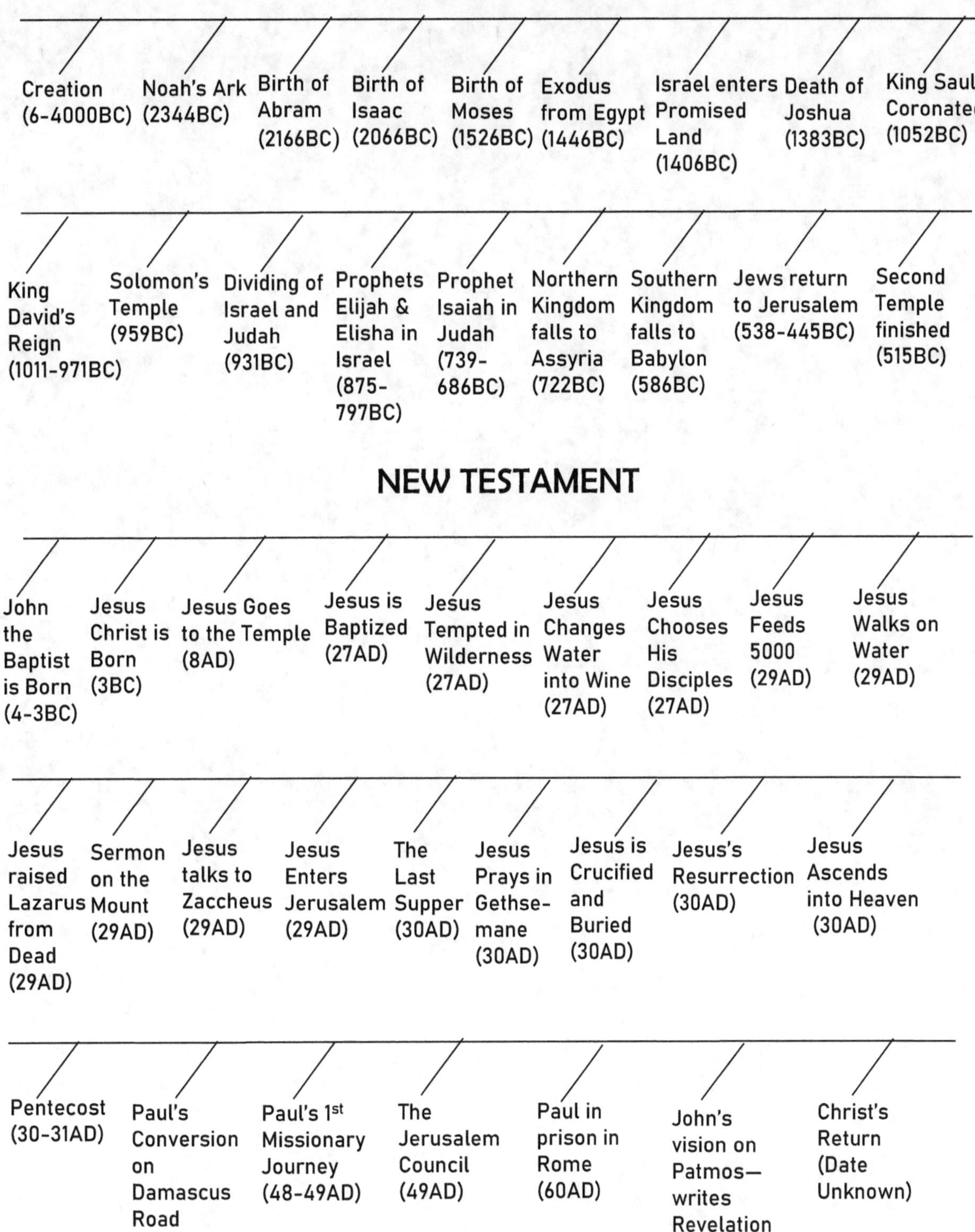

www.ingramcontent.com/pod-product-compliance
Lightning Source LLC
Chambersburg PA
CBHW060202120726
48004CB00007B/1654